HEAL ME, O LORD!

Powerful Scriptural
Keys to Receive
Your Healing
Touch From God

DAVID & BARBARA
CERULLO

Heal Me, O Lord
by David and Barbara Cerullo
Copyright ©2011

Published by Inspiration Ministries
P.O. Box 7750
Charlotte, NC 28241 USA
803-578-1899
inspiration.org

ISBN 978-1-936177-09-7

Printed in the United States of America.

Contents

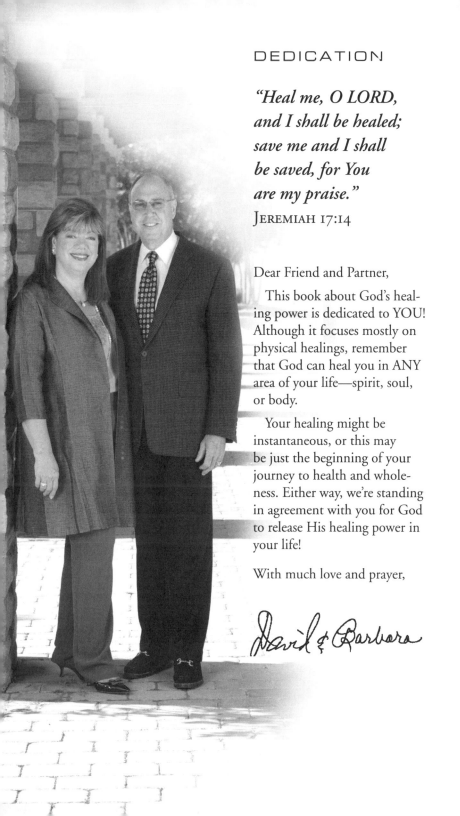

DEDICATION

"Heal me, O LORD, and I shall be healed; save me and I shall be saved, for You are my praise."
JEREMIAH 17:14

Dear Friend and Partner,

This book about God's healing power is dedicated to YOU! Although it focuses mostly on physical healings, remember that God can heal you in ANY area of your life—spirit, soul, or body.

Your healing might be instantaneous, or this may be just the beginning of your journey to health and wholeness. Either way, we're standing in agreement with you for God to release His healing power in your life!

With much love and prayer,

David & Barbara

Six Steps to Receive Your Healing

STEP 1 — ELIMINATE ANY HINDRANCES

Before you approach God for His healing touch, make sure to deal with any hindrances that could block His blessings. Ask the Holy Spirit to convict you of such things as unbelief...unforgiveness...pride...sin...generational sins... poor choices...and fear. Then ask Him to relieve you of anxiety and stress as you prepare the way for His healing power to flow in your spirit, soul, and body.

STEP 2 — WORSHIP

During one of the great battles in Israel, King Jehoshaphat's army was so outnumbered by the enemy that they didn't stand a chance (2 Chronicles 20). What did Jehoshaphat do? God told him to appoint singers to go out ahead of the army to praise the Lord.

The Bible records the miraculous result: *"When they began singing and praising, the LORD set ambushes against the sons of Ammon, Moab, and Mount Seir, which were come against Judah; and they were defeated"* (v. 22).

What a lesson! When we choose to worship the Lord when faced with poor health or other challenging circumstances, God gives us victory and smites the enemy on our behalf! So when you're overwhelmed by a health crisis, start giving the Lord honor and praise.

When you worship God, miracles happen! Worship will help you completely surrender your spirit, soul, and body to the Lord. It signals your recognition that He alone holds the answers to your health and that you can't resolve your problems in your own strength.

STEP 3 — PRAY THE WORD

Isaiah 55:11 reveals the amazing power of God's Word: *"So shall My Word be that goes forth from My mouth; it shall not return to Me void, but it shall accomplish what I please, and it shall prosper in the thing for which I sent it."* When our prayers are based on His Word, God promises that what we're asking Him to do will be accomplished.

Ask the Holy Spirit to lead you to Scripture passages concerning your health and wellbeing.

Many of the verses in this booklet make excellent prayers, and the Lord will also show you others.

Choose Bible promises on healing and personalize them. Here's an example based on Isaiah 43:1-2:

The LORD, my Creator, says that I am not to be afraid about my health, because He has redeemed me, spirit, soul, and body. He has called me by name, and I am His! When I pass through the waters and feel as though I'm drowning in my sickness, He has promised to be with me and save me. When it seems as though I'm walking through fires of disease, I will not be scorched. Because of His love and protection, the flames of adversity won't burn me. Amen!

Pray Scripture verses like this over yourself throughout the day to encourage and strengthen you when you're feeling sick and weary and are tempted to be hopeless about your health and healing. The Bible advises us, *"Death and life are in the power of the tongue"* (Proverbs 18:21). By praying the Word over yourself, you will be praying God's life over your spirit, soul, and body!

STEP 4 — WAGE SPIRITUAL WAR

Be aware of Satan's strategies to rob you of your health (John 10:10), and make sure you put on the whole armor of God to resist him (Ephesians 6:14-17). You can overcome the enemy's attacks by the mighty spiritual weapons God has given you (2 Corinthians 10:4).

The Word declares, *"The Son of God appeared for this purpose, to destroy the works of the devil"* (1 John 3:8 NASB). Through Christ, you have the power to defeat Satan's attacks against your health!

When your life is submitted to God's authority, you can tell the devil, "Stay out of my life!"—and he must flee (James 4:7).

STEP 5 — ASK GOD FOR WISDOM

As you are getting advice and making decisions about your health, it's imperative that you follow Solomon's guidance and *"get wisdom"* (Proverbs 4:7). The world, your doctor, and well-meaning family and friends may all have opinions about what you should do when you need healing. But instead of blindly following every offer of health advice, you must ask God for His wisdom.

When making decisions on your health, a good rule of thumb is to let God's peace steer your heart: *"Let the peace of Christ rule in your hearts, to which indeed you were called in one body; and be thankful"* (Colossians 3:15 NASB).

So BE WISE! Don't make a major health decision until you have peace in your heart. Don't be in a hurry to move until you know God has given you His wisdom. Sometimes you have to WAIT for God's instructions and His healing touch. While He may give you an instantaneous miracle, at other times the healing will be more gradual.

God wants to heal you! He's your Jehovah-Rapha—the God who heals ALL your diseases (Psalm 103:3). But if you don't receive your healing right away, remember these words from Jeremiah: *"It is good that a man should both hope and wait quietly for the salvation of the LORD"* (Lamentations 3:26).

STEP 6 — REACH OUT AND TOUCH HIM BY FAITH

Today, I encourage you to follow the example of the woman who had suffered with a hemorrhage for 12 long years (Mark 5:24-34). She knew she would be healed if she could just touch the edge of Jesus' robe.

The same is true for YOU today! Jesus is with you right now. Reach out and touch Him by faith, asking Him for the healing you need!

MY PRAYER FOR YOU:

Heavenly Father, thank You that because of Your great love, You want to heal Your child and make them whole in their spirit, mind, and body. I ask for Your healing power to touch them mightily today. Wrap Your loving arms around them and let them feel Your presence and Your peace.

I proclaim today in Jesus' mighty name that every healing promise in Your Word is true for them. Make them a tremendous testimony of Your love and healing power. In Jesus' name. Amen.

My friend, be healed today in the name of Jesus!

HEAL ME, O LORD!

31 Daily Devotionals About God's Healing Power

DAY 1

The God Who Heals

"If you will give earnest heed to the voice of the LORD your God, and do what is right in His sight, and give ear to His commandments, and keep all His statutes, I will put none of the diseases on you which I have put on the Egyptians; for I, the LORD, am your healer."

Exodus 15:26 NASB

"**Y**our healer" is how God described Himself to Moses. This defined His character and declared His commitment. In fact, He promised to free His people from all diseases. But there were conditions to His promise. If they wanted healing, they must heed His voice, do what was right, obey His commandments, and keep His statutes.

These principles apply in our lives as well. Although God is still our healer, it can be easy to doubt this truth. Many in the world tell us there is no God. They say it's foolish to believe in healing, and claim that prayer doesn't work. Even some Christians are skeptical, doubting that God truly heals today.

Nevertheless, God has not changed, and He declares that He's our healer!

But there are conditions for us, just as the Lord told Moses. We, too, need to listen carefully to His voice, fill our minds with His Word, and declare His promises to be true.

We also must *do what is right* in His eyes. We can't expect healing and blessing if we walk in sin or go our own way.

When we know and obey God's Word, He helps shape our lives. He enables us to be more productive, to have more impact, and to have faith!

Today, remember this truth: God still heals. Declare this promise for you and your family! Keep His commandments, and let His Word shape your thoughts and actions. Don't let doubt rob you of His desire to heal you. Pray expectantly, boldly, and confidently. Let faith rise in your heart. He has said it: *"I am your healer."*

PRAYER:

Father, thank You for being my healer! I believe You for health in my life. I commit these people who need healing to You: _____. Thank You for healing them! In Jesus' name. Amen.

HEALING KEY:

GOD IS YOUR HEALER!

DAY 2

God's Desire for Your Health

"Beloved, I pray that in all respects you may prosper and be in good health, just as your soul prospers."

3 John 1:2 NASB

What is God's desire for us? There can be no clearer statement than these words written by John. He presented a truth that is simple but overwhelming: God wants us to prosper!

First, He wants us to prosper spiritually—being strong and mature in our faith, and receiving all the blessings He's prepared for us. He also wants us to prosper in our finances...our relationships...our families...and our businesses.

And John specifically says God wants us to *"be in good health"*—experiencing wellness in our body, mind, and emotions.

Some people find it difficult to believe these promises are true. They find it easier to think like the world, live with doubt, and be victims instead of victors.

But Jesus taught that He came so His followers *"may have life, and that they may have it more abundantly"* (John 10:10). If we understand the full purpose of salvation, we see that God wants us to live in this abundant life all the time!

The Lord doesn't want us to be defeated, but victorious. He doesn't want us to be sick or in pain, but in divine health. He has promised to meet our needs *"according to His riches in glory by Christ Jesus"* (Philippians 4:19).

Today, think about God's desire for you. Your needs may seem overwhelming. Someone may have told you there's no hope for your situation. But don't be discouraged. Remember that you serve the God of all creation. And don't allow the thief to steal your victory!

Right now, declare this truth: God wants you to *"be in good health, just as your soul prospers."* Praise Him, for this is His will for you! Receive His full blessings—health, wisdom, prosperity, freedom from fear and worry, and an abundant life. Don't accept anything less!

PRAYER:

Father, thank You that You want me to prosper in all things and to be in health. I will not doubt but believe Your Word! I receive Your prosperity and health! In Jesus' name. Amen.

HEALING KEY:

GOD WANTS YOU TO PROSPER AND BE IN HEALTH!

DAY 3

Today's Bible Reading: *Isaiah 53*
His Stripes

"He was wounded for our transgressions, He was bruised for our iniquities; the chastisement for our peace was upon Him, and by His stripes we are healed."

Isaiah 53:5 NASB

Some thought of Jesus as merely a teacher or wise man. When He taught, they pressed around Him, eager to hear His words.

Some thought of Him as a miracle-worker. They rejoiced when He healed the sick and marveled when He opened the eyes of the blind.

For these and other reasons, the crowds united in loud praise as Jesus approached Jerusalem for the last time. They shouted, *"Blessed is the King who comes in the name of the Lord"* (Luke 19:38).

Yet, as Isaiah prophesied, there was another side to His earthly life. In addition to being the *"Wonderful Counselor, Mighty God, Eternal Father, Prince of Peace"* (Isaiah 9:6), the Messiah also would come as the Suffering Servant.

While some loved Him, others *"despised and rejected"* Him (v. 3 NKJV). Ultimately, He was wounded and *"bruised for our iniquities."* Although He lived a sinless life, He was scourged and given stripes by Roman soldiers. Then He was crucified on a brutal Cross.

It was no coincidence that He died during Passover, for He came to be the *"Lamb of God who takes away the sin of the world"* (John 1:29). He became our Passover Lamb.

Today, remember that Jesus is your Passover Lamb! He died for you! He was despised and forsaken…for you! He was wounded for your transgressions, and His stripes provided healing…for you!

Are you or someone you know suffering from sickness or disease? Don't give up. Turn to Jesus, and have faith in Him. He will not disappoint you. He has experienced pain. He knows what you're going through. He is ready to comfort, heal, and change you forever. He is your Messiah…the Lamb of God. Trust Him, and believe His promises.

PRAYER:

Dear Lord Jesus, thank You for being the Lamb of God and dying for my sins. I commit these people to You: _____. I declare that by Your stripes they are healed! In Your name. Amen.

HEALING KEY:

BY JESUS' STRIPES, YOU ARE HEALED!

DAY 4

Complete Healing and Forgiveness

"Bless the LORD, O my soul, and all that is within me, bless His holy name... Who heals all your diseases... Who satisfies your years with good things, so that your youth is renewed like the eagle."

Psalm 103:1-5 NASB

David's heart overflowed with thanksgiving and praise. As he realized all that God had done for him, he couldn't help but bless His holy name! David knew that God doesn't heal just some of our diseases—He heals all of them! God doesn't forgive just some sins—He forgives all of them!

The Lord wants us to experience a life of blessing, for He redeems our lives *"from the pit"* and crowns us *"with lovingkindness and compassion."* He is able to give us satisfaction and fulfillment, and we can be renewed constantly, just *"like the eagle."*

We do not serve a God who does things only part way. He's a God of healing and restoration, forgiveness and power! Nothing is too difficult for Him. Nothing!

Right now, no matter what you've done or what problems you face, think about the promises in God's Word. They are true for you! If you've made mistakes or committed sins, confess them. He is ready to forgive you. Remember what He's done in your life, and declare His promises—starting with Psalm 103.

If you have any sickness, addictions, or infirmities, cry out to God. He's the God who *"heals all your diseases."* He is available to redeem your life from destruction...to crown you with lovingkindness...to satisfy you with good things...and to renew your life like an eagle.

Don't hold back or accept less than God's desire for you. Refuse to accept defeat or be ruled by doubt. Instead, be bold, confident, and filled with faith.

And don't forget to praise Him. He is worthy!

PRAYER:
Father, I declare that Your promises are true for me! Thank You for healing my diseases. Thank You for redeeming my life. Thank You for renewing me. In Jesus' name. Amen.

HEALING KEY:
DECLARE THAT GOD HEALS ALL YOUR DISEASES!

DAY 5

Healing Every Disease

"Jesus was going throughout all Galilee, teaching in their synagogues and proclaiming the gospel of the kingdom, and healing every kind of disease and every kind of sickness among the people."

Matthew 4:23 NASB

Think of all the problems people faced! There were all types of sickness and disease. Some were minor, some major. Some cases were terminal, while others seemed trivial. There were both mental and physical ailments. Some people had suffered for years and given up hope. Others had been abused or beaten.

Jesus encountered people who were demon-possessed or afflicted with epilepsy. Some were paralyzed, while others were blind or deaf. Some simply were confused or troubled.

As Jesus traveled through Galilee, people brought the sick to Him. No matter what sickness or problem they faced, Jesus healed them all!

Some people believe that this kind of healing no longer takes place. But the Bible tells us Jesus is *"the same yesterday, today, and forever"* (Hebrews 13:8). He's the same as He was that day in Galilee. He's the same Savior who healed every disease and solved every kind of problem.

The Bible even shows us that healing was central to the Gospel proclamation, for Jesus healed and delivered people as He was *"proclaiming the Gospel of the kingdom."*

Right now, you may be facing health issues. Perhaps you feel confusion or mental strain. Or maybe you're feeling emotionally unsettled. People may have told you that your situation is hopeless.

Don't be discouraged or afraid. Instead of giving up, picture yourself as one of the people who came to Jesus in Galilee, filled with expectation and faith. Believe that He can heal every sickness and every disease. He can provide for every need you face.

Accept His healing! Receive His power. Believe!

PRAYER:

Dear Lord Jesus, I bring my needs and the needs of these people to You: _____. I believe that You can heal every disease and solve every problem. In Your name. Amen.

HEALING KEY:

JESUS HEALED EVERY KIND OF DISEASE AND SICKNESS!

DAY 6

Destroying the Works of the Devil

"The one who practices sin is of the devil; for the devil has sinned from the beginning. The Son of God appeared for this purpose, to destroy the works of the devil."

1 John 3:8 NASB

Right now, the devil and his demonic forces are at work in the world. As they have throughout history, they are spreading confusion and deception, tempting people to sin and believe their lies, attacking families and marriages, dividing churches and causing violence, bringing oppression and disease.

These satanic forces can seem overwhelming, even invincible. But the Bible tells us that Jesus came to destroy these works and give us victory over all their attacks.

Jesus did not come to tolerate the works of the devil, or just make a dent in the works of darkness. No. He came to destroy these works! The word translated "works" literally means business, employment, or anything else in which someone is occupied. This means Jesus came to demolish and destroy anything the devil is doing. Anything!

You can personalize this verse by applying it to you and your family. Jesus came to eliminate any influence of the devil in your life! Satan might be seeking to confuse your mind, discourage you, or cause you to doubt God. He may be trying to disrupt your life or tempt you to accept less than what God has prepared for you. Or perhaps he has trapped you in unhealthy lifestyles or habits, causing you to experience sickness and disease.

Right now, turn your heart and mind toward God. Consider any ways the devil might be influencing you. Then recognize that God sent Jesus to destroy the works of the devil in each and every area of your life. Declare and receive His complete and total victory.

Don't tolerate evil or compromise! Refuse to allow Satan and his demonic forces to have any influence in your life. With Jesus, you can live in victory and freedom!

PRAYER:

Father, thank You for sending Jesus to destroy the work of the devil. I bind his power to influence my life and my family. I believe You for total victory. In Jesus' name. Amen.

HEALING KEY:

BELIEVE THAT JESUS CAME TO DESTROY THE WORKS OF THE DEVIL!

DAY 7

The Power of the Resurrection

"Do not be afraid; for I know that you are looking for Jesus who has been crucified. He is not here, for He has risen, just as He said."

Matthew 28:5 NASB

Today, many people want to remove the supernatural elements from Jesus' life. They want to reduce Him to nothing more than a wise man or a good teacher. Some want to make the celebration of the Resurrection into nothing more than a cultural holiday—a time for parties and lighthearted fun, a day of costumes and ceremonies, even a season of shopping.

For the Christian, however, the Resurrection is the ultimate expression of God's supernatural power in action, the day when the impossible became possible, when Jesus was raised from the dead!

Jesus' Resurrection was a complete surprise to the disciples. Their initial reaction was fear. They were mystified. Could it possibly be true? What could it mean?

When Jesus rose from the grave, He unleashed spiritual dynamite. His death and Resurrection destroyed the hold of Satan, gave us unquenchable hope, and shattered the barriers that separated people from God.

The Resurrection was so important to Paul that he said, *"If Christ is not risen, your faith is futile; you are still in your sins"* (1 Corinthians 15:17). He prayed we might *"know the power of his resurrection"* (Philippians 3:10), and he wrote, *"If the Spirit of Him who raised Jesus from the dead dwells in you, He who raised Christ from the dead will also give life to your mortal bodies through His Spirit who dwells in you"* (Romans 8:11).

That same power is available to you…right now! God can give life to your mortal body. He can give you health and power, wisdom and resources—things that seem impossible!

Today, celebrate the Resurrection of Jesus. Like the disciples, marvel at this overwhelming miracle. And remember: He still performs miracles! This Resurrection power can be real for anyone…for you! Jesus has risen! If God can raise the dead, He can do anything!

PRAYER:

Father, thank You that Jesus rose from the dead. Touch my life and my body with that same Resurrection power. I rejoice in Your salvation! In Jesus' name. Amen.

HEALING KEY:

GOD HAS GIVEN YOU ACCESS TO RESURRECTION POWER!

DAY 8

Knowing Jesus

"Whatever things were gain to me, those things I have counted as loss for the sake of Christ...that I may know Him and the power of His resurrection and the fellowship of His sufferings, being conformed to His death; in order that I may attain to the resurrection from the dead."

Philippians 3:7-11 NASB

Millions of people say they believe Jesus rose from the dead. But many don't live as though this makes a difference. Some may have read about *"the power of His resurrection,"* but they've never experienced this power in their own lives. Some may believe it's available for others, but they don't know how to appropriate this power for themselves.

Paul had experienced this power himself and witnessed it in lives throughout the world. He had seen the miraculous changes it made. He said that in order to receive this Resurrection power, we must lay aside everything else and place Jesus first in our lives. This requires a total commitment—spending time with Him, reading His Word, and seeking Him with our whole heart.

Each day, we all face many distractions. It can be easy to focus our attention on daily needs and desires, temporary pleasures or problems. But God offers us so much more! He offers the very Resurrection power of Jesus to change our lives.

Instead of being dominated by our flesh, we must live by faith in Jesus. Our goal must be to *"know Him and the power of His resurrection."* Everything else must be like *"rubbish"* so we can *"gain Christ and be found in Him."* We must realize that we have no righteousness of our own and need to receive God's forgiveness and power through faith.

Today, ask God to help you know Jesus more deeply than ever before. Make Him first in your life. Then experience His Resurrection power!

PRAYER:

Father, I count everything in my life as loss so that I can know Jesus as my Lord. May I experience the transforming power of His Resurrection. In His name. Amen.

HEALING KEY:

GIVE JESUS FIRST PLACE, AND EXPERIENCE THE POWER OF HIS RESURRECTION!

DAY 9

Today's Bible Reading: *Deuteronomy 8*
God's Desire for You

"You shall remember the LORD your God, for it is He who is giving you power to make wealth, that He may confirm His covenant which He swore to your fathers."

Deuteronomy 8:18 NASB

Before the children of Israel entered the Promised Land, Moses taught them an important insight about the nature of God. He said it was God Himself *"who is giving you power to make wealth."* They could not succeed on their own. They needed to depend on God.

A whole series of blessings would flow into their lives…if they obeyed His commands and trusted in Him. He would grant them health and favor, blessing and protection.

This principle still is true. It is repeated throughout the Bible. For example, the Bible tells us God wants us to *"prosper and be in good health"* (3 John 1:2). And Peter writes that *"His divine power has granted to us everything pertaining to life and godliness"* (2 Peter 1:3)—everything!

The Bible cannot be any clearer: God wants to bless us and give us divine health. Some people have a hard time believing these truths, but this is what God's Word declares.

Are you limiting God because of negative thinking? Are you even expecting problems and confessing doubt instead of confessing God's promises? Do you question if God truly wants to bless and prosper you?

Take the limits off your thinking. Remember you serve the God who created the universe. His Word declares that, with Him, nothing is impossible!

But also remember that you will Reap what you Sow. You have choices to make with the time, talent, and treasure you've been given—choices about how you spend your time, what thoughts you think, and which things you allow into your mind. Be careful!

If you want God's health and blessing in every area, seek to be a good steward and a faithful servant. Have faith that He will bless you and grant you His health and favor.

PRAYER:

Father, thank You that You want me to experience health and prosperity. I want to receive Your blessings in everything I do. I dedicate my life and resources to You. In Jesus' name. Amen.

HEALING KEY:

GOD HAS GRANTED YOU EVERYTHING PERTAINING TO LIFE AND GODLINESS.

DAY 10

Surpassingly Great Power

"I pray that the eyes of your heart may be enlightened, so that you will know what is the hope of His calling, what are the riches of the glory of His inheritance in the saints, and what is the surpassing greatness of His power toward us who believe."

Ephesians 1:18-19 NASB

Our jobs. Families and friendships. The news. Rumors and gossip. Hobbies and interests. Pleasures and desires. Entertainment and our social lives. Shopping and dining. Finances and bills.

These kinds of things tend to occupy so much of our daily schedule. How easily our energies can be consumed with these activities! Problem after problem, and project after project, pass through our lives. It can seem like we're on an unending treadmill, never really going anywhere.

We can become so preoccupied that we fail to grasp the spiritual riches God has made available to us. We can accept a mediocre faith and be content with a life filled with problems and defeat. But that is not God's desire for us.

God offers us *"a rich and glorious inheritance."* Just think! Incredibly great power is available to us…if we believe in Him. In fact, *"this is the same mighty power that raised Christ from the dead and seated him in the place of honor at God's right hand in the heavenly realms"* (vs. 19-20 NLT). He wants us to share that same power, right now!

God also wants us to know the hope to which He has called us. Because of Jesus, we have hope when we face monumental problems, when nothing seems to be going right, when we're discouraged or afraid, when we don't seem to have enough resources, or when we're experiencing sickness.

Don't be content with less than God's best for you. Ask Him to give you a fresh grasp of the full dimension of His Resurrection power—and expect His power to be unleashed in your life.

PRAYER:

Father, help me to know Your rich blessings and the hope You've called me to. Release Your power in my life. I want Your fullness! In Jesus' name. Amen.

HEALING KEY:

SEE THE SURPASSING GREATNESS OF THE POWER GOD HAS GIVEN YOU.

DAY 11

A Name Above Every Name

"…He raised Him from the dead and seated Him at His right hand in the heavenly places, far above all rule and authority and power and dominion, and every name that is named, not only in this age but also in the one to come. And He put all things in subjection under His feet."

Ephesians 1:20-22 NASB

Many Christians do not experience the power of God in their lives. Some simply assume they have no power. Others become discouraged and wonder if God has forgotten them. Many never believe they can escape their problems or experience victory.

But Paul had a message for all of us: We serve a great God! He's a God who has given great power to everyone who believes, and He wants us to have faith and live with boldness and confidence.

As he wrote his letter to the Ephesians, Paul tried to help these Believers grasp God's greatness and the overwhelming power He's made available to His people. This same power raised Jesus from the dead and flows from His presence at the right hand of the Father, where He is *"far above all rule and authority and power and dominion, and every name that is named."* Think about that: All things will always be under His feet—not just now, but forever!

Paul writes that the name of Jesus is greater than any other name! That means His authority is greater than any disease or problem…any project or company…any obstacle or person. He is above anything, anyone, and everything. And because we are His Body, all of these things are now under us as well…through Christ!

If you believe in Jesus, this great power is available to you. Right now!

Ask God to help you understand this truth. Confess what His Word says, and believe that it's true! Don't be satisfied with less than He desires for you. You don't have to live in weakness. Become bold in your faith and belief. Receive the power He has given you!

PRAYER:

Father, help me to grasp the exceedingly great power You have given me. Help me to exercise this power and dominion so I can glorify You and live in victory. In Jesus' name. Amen.

HEALING KEY:

JESUS' NAME IS ABOVE ANY PROBLEM AND ANY OTHER NAME.

DAY 12

A God Without Limits

"'Sir, I have no man to put me into the pool when the water is stirred up, but while I am coming, another steps down before me.' Jesus said to him, 'Get up, pick up your pallet and walk.'...So the Jews were saying to the man who was cured, 'It is the Sabbath, and it is not permissible for you to carry your pallet.'"

John 5:7-10 NASB

This paralyzed man at the Pool of Bethesda believed that God could heal, yet he placed limits on God. Yes, he thought God might be able to heal him, but only after the water was *"stirred."* Only then could a healing take place, and only one person could be healed at a time. He couldn't imagine that God could do anything, at any time.

This man developed his thinking because of rules imposed by Jewish leaders. These men believed that they knew when and how God would act. Since it was the Sabbath, they concluded that healing was impossible. And they enforced their rigid rules on everyone, causing their thinking to be limited.

But Jesus wanted them to understand that He had authority in every situation. He wasn't bound by any limits. So He spoke, and the paralyzed man was instantly healed. This seemed shocking and inappropriate to the religious authorities, but Jesus had a greater purpose: demonstrating that God was sovereign in every situation.

Jesus knows how easy it is for us to be like those Jewish leaders, thinking we have everything figured out and assuming we know what God can and can't do. But Jesus wanted us to realize He has no limits. He can act at any time of His choosing, and He looks for people with the faith to believe in this limitless power.

Today, remember there are no problems too big for Jesus. No situations are too hopeless. No obstacles can stand before Him.

He is present with you right now! Believe Him for healing, wisdom, direction—whatever you need!

PRAYER:
Dear Lord Jesus, I commit these needs to You: _____. I believe nothing is too big or too hard for You. Thank You for miracles in my life. In Your name. Amen.

HEALING KEY:
DON'T IMPOSE LIMITS ON THE LIMITLESS GOD.

DAY 13

Today's Bible Reading: *John 5*
Becoming Totally Whole

"A man was there who had been ill for thirty-eight years… 'Do you wish to get well?'…Jesus said to him, 'Get up, pick up your pallet and walk.' Immediately the man became well, and picked up his pallet and began to walk."

John 5:5-9 NASB

This man had been sick for 38 years. He thought his only hope was for the water to be *"stirred up,"* when one person at the Pool of Bethesda could be healed. But it never seemed his turn, and he lost all hope. It seemed he would remain paralyzed forever.

Then he met Jesus. When the Lord spoke words of healing, the man instantly became whole and was able to walk for the first time in 38 years! Jesus wanted the man to realize He was concerned about every part of his life—wholeness for his body and forgiveness for his sins.

Throughout His ministry, Jesus constantly brought people total health. Those who came to Him in faith weren't allowed to remain sick or depressed, lonely or poor, discouraged or afraid.

Jesus brought people the full impact of God's Kingdom—providing wisdom and forgiveness, deliverance and healing. In addition to forgiveness, His Gospel offered people an abundant life (John 10:10), healing for every disease (Matthew 4:24), and an impartation of power and authority (Luke 9:1).

Sadly, many Christians today are content with sickness, defeat, and depression. They tolerate much less than God's desire for them.

How about you? Are there problems you've faced for a long time? Are there habits you can't seem to shake? Do you have nagging health issues? Are you feeling discouraged?

Remember that God sent Jesus so you could be totally whole. You don't have to suffer with sin or sickness, or be afraid or worried.

Don't be content with anything less than God's best for you. Call on Him right now. He has promised to *"supply all your needs according to his riches in glory in Christ Jesus"* (Philippians 4:19). Let Him make you totally whole!

PRAYER:
Father, thank You that You want me to be whole. I commit every need to you. I believe You for health for my body, wholeness for my mind, and strength for my spirit. In Jesus' name. Amen.

HEALING KEY:
GOD WANTS YOU TO BE TOTALLY WHOLE—SPIRIT, SOUL, AND BODY.

DAY 14

Turnaround for a Lame Man

"A man who had been lame from his mother's womb was being carried along…to beg alms of those who were entering the temple…Peter…fixed his gaze on him and said…'I do not possess silver and gold, but what I do have I give to you: In the name of Jesus Christ the Nazarene—walk!'"

Acts 3:2-6 NASB

The man had nothing, and his future looked bleak. Lame throughout his life, he spent most days simply begging from those who entered the temple. Their handouts provided his daily bread. Certainly he believed in God, but he never even considered the possibility that God would care enough about his situation to heal him.

But Peter knew that nothing was impossible with God. When he spoke the word of faith, the cripple was instantly healed. Filled with joy, he walked, jumped, and praised God! His whole life turned around in a mere moment.

Many people approach life like this crippled man. Feeling trapped and hopeless, they're convinced nothing will ever change. They believe they're sentenced to suffer forever with sickness or poverty, failure or defeat, doubt or depression.

Even Christians can have this attitude. While they know Bible stories like the healing of this lame man, they can't imagine God's power intervening in their circumstances and changing their lives.

Today, you may face situations that seem hopeless. You may have problems you can't seem to solve. You or someone you know may be facing a serious health issue.

But no matter what you are dealing with, remember that God can supply your needs. And He also can make you like Peter, able to bring His healing and health to others.

God is with you, right now. His Word is true. Be ready to step out in faith. In a mere moment, He can turn your entire life around. And He can use you to impact others with His Kingdom power!

PRAYER:
Father, give me boldness to believe that all Your promises are true for me. Open doors for me to speak Your Word and impact others with Your healing power. In Jesus' name. Amen.

HEALING KEY:
GOD CAN TURN YOUR LIFE AROUND IN A MERE MOMENT.

DAY 15

Given Perfect Health

"On the basis of faith in His name, it is the name of Jesus which has strengthened this man whom you see and know; and the faith which comes through Him has given him this perfect health in the presence of you all."

Acts 3:16 NASB

What happened when God intervened in the life of this lame man? Did he become a little better? Did God take care of just some of his problems? No. The man was given *"perfect health."* The Greek word (used here for the only time in the Bible) means to be completely whole, with all members of the body healthy and ready to be used.

What an amazing miracle! This man had been lame his entire life. Every day, for many years, he sat *"at the gate of the temple which is called Beautiful, in order to beg alms of those who were entering the temple"* (v. 2). He had few expectations and little hope.

But Peter and John knew there was no limit to what God could do. Filled with faith and God's power, Peter gave a simple, direct command: *"In the name of Jesus Christ the Nazarene—walk!"* The man instantly rose to his feet: *"Immediately his feet and his ankles were strengthened. With a leap he stood upright and began to walk."* He entered the temple, *"walking and leaping and praising God"* (vs. 7-8). He was a new man, completely whole! Overwhelmed, he jumped with uninhibited joy, just like a child.

Today, remember that you serve the same God who performed this miracle. He is the God who can do all things. Do you face problems? Health issues? Financial difficulties? Relationship problems? Emotional uncertainty?

Don't place limits on what God can do for you. He can do anything and everything. Not just small things, but BIG things, amazing things—perfect health, complete wholeness, total solutions to your problems!

PRAYER:
Father, I commit these needs to You: _____. Thank You for offering me healing and health! Forgive me for limiting You. I believe that nothing is impossible. In Jesus' name. Amen.

HEALING KEY:
IN THE NAME OF JESUS, ALL THINGS ARE POSSIBLE.

DAY 16

Filled With the Holy Spirit

"Let it be known to all of you and to all the people of Israel, that by the name of Jesus Christ the Nazarene, whom you crucified, whom God raised from the dead—by this name this man stands here before you in good health."

Acts 4:10 NASB

After being filled with the Holy Spirit, Peter experienced a new kind of power. Before being filled with the Spirit, he had even denied knowing Jesus. But now, empowered by the Spirit, his life was transformed. Speaking in Jesus' name, he was no longer tentative, but bold. He had authority, and mighty miracles could take place.

Seeing a lame man, Peter said, *"In the name of Jesus of Nazareth start walking."* The result was immediate. Peter *"took him by the right hand and lifted him, and his feet and ankles instantly grew strong, and at once he leaped to his feet and started walking; then he went into the temple with them, walking, leaping, and praising God"* (Acts 3:6-8).

The news of this miracle spread throughout Jerusalem. People were amazed. But Peter made it clear to everyone: The man was healed because of the Resurrection power of God.

That same Resurrection power is available to you. All who believe in Jesus have access to that power through His name and the presence of His Holy Spirit. That power can cure sicknesses that seem incurable, overcome emotional trauma and stress, defeat worry and fear, end confusion, and solve overwhelming problems.

No matter who you are, you can have immediate access to God because of Jesus. His power is real and available for you right now. The Holy Spirit can transform your life!

Today, don't let human weaknesses rule your life. Declare that Jesus is your Lord. Seek to be filled with the Spirit. Seek an outpouring of His Resurrection power in your life. Let Him pray through you, teach through you, and give you boldness and power, wisdom and insight. Let Him use you to bring healing and deliverance to others. Remember: With God, nothing is impossible!

PRAYER:

Father, I commit these situations to You: _____. Thank You for releasing Your Resurrection power. I will not doubt, but will trust in You. In Jesus' name. Amen.

HEALING KEY:

BE FILLED WITH THE SPIRIT AND RECEIVE THE RESURRECTION POWER OF GOD.

DAY 17

Today's Bible Reading: *Acts 8*
Releasing the Spirit's Power

"The apostles in Jerusalem…sent them Peter and John, who came down and prayed for them that they might receive the Holy Spirit…Then they began laying their hands on them, and they were receiving the Holy Spirit."

Acts 8:14-17 NASB

Miracles took place and people responded with great joy when Philip proclaimed Christ in Samaria. But the apostles in Jerusalem realized these new Believers needed the power of the Holy Spirit. Peter and John were sent so they could receive Him.

The disciples knew the importance of the Holy Spirit. Even after spending years with Jesus, something had been missing in their lives until the day of Pentecost, when they were filled with the Spirit and everything changed.

These timid, tentative men suddenly became powerful preachers and dynamic witnesses. Suddenly, they could heal the sick, and they displayed a new depth of wisdom.

As they brought the Gospel to others, they realized that everyone needed the power of the Holy Spirit. Just as Jesus promised (Acts 1:8), they had received power when the Holy Spirit came upon them (Acts 2:4). They knew they were given this power to be His witnesses and change the lives of others.

The disciples understood what Jesus had been saying when He promised that the Holy Spirit would be their Helper and would teach them *"all things"* (John 14:26). They realized that the Spirit would guide them *"into all the truth"* and even reveal *"what is to come"* (John 16:13).

Remember that this same Holy Spirit is available to you, right now. You can't change the world or impact lives with just your human strength or ability. You need the power of the Holy Spirit.

God's Spirit can transform you in supernatural ways. He can give you a powerful prayer life and enable you to perform miracles. He can give you the fruit of the Spirit and touch your body with health and healing.

Today, wait on the Spirit. Listen to the Spirit. Be filled with the Spirit.

PRAYER:
Holy Spirit, help me to be sensitive to Your presence. Fill me. Teach me. Use me. I surrender my life to Your control. Flow through me to change lives. In Jesus' name. Amen.

HEALING KEY:
LET THE HOLY SPIRIT TRANSFORM YOUR LIFE AND GIVE YOU POWER.

27

DAY 18

Boldness to Believe

"In Iconium…a large number of people believed…But the Jews who disbelieved stirred up the minds of the Gentiles and embittered them against the brethren. Therefore they spent a long time there speaking boldly with reliance upon the Lord, who was testifying to the word of His grace, granting that signs and wonders be done by their hands."

Acts 14:1-3 NASB

Many people in the city of Iconium responded to the Gospel message. But as a result, there was a wave of opposition. Disbelieving Jews created trouble, and some Gentiles became *"embittered."* However, instead of watering down their ministry, Paul and Barnabas continued to speak *"boldly,"* relying on the Lord to protect and defend them. Rather than cowering in fear or giving in to compromise, they had faith to believe that God would do *"signs and wonders."* As a result, many miracles took place.

Yes, they faced resistance, opposition, and persecution. But they didn't stop or run away. They refused to back down or change their message. Instead, they experienced new levels of boldness and power. Eventually, Paul and Barnabas had to depart Iconium, but they left a witness that had made a mark on the people.

In our lives, we can expect opposition. Some will resist and reject the Gospel. We sometimes will be ridiculed and mocked. People will attack us and say the Bible isn't true, prayers can't be answered, and miracles don't happen today. But we can learn from how Paul and Barnabas acted in Iconium.

Don't be surprised if you face opposition, yet don't let it provoke fear and worry in your heart. Like Paul and Barnabas, continue moving forward in faith. Be bold, and put your faith into action.

Be an instrument God can use to demonstrate His power. Believe Him for miracles, signs, and wonders, and be ready to speak healing into the lives of others. God wants to use you to change lives!

PRAYER:

Father, demonstrate Your power through me. Touch other people by doing signs and wonders through my life. Help me to be a bold witness for You. In Jesus' name. Amen.

HEALING KEY:

GOD STILL PERFORMS SIGNS AND WONDERS.

DAY 19

The Prayer of Faith

"Is anyone among you sick? Then he must call for the elders of the church and they are to pray over him, anointing him with oil in the name of the Lord; and the prayer offered in faith will restore the one who is sick, and the Lord will raise him up, and if he has committed sins, they will be forgiven him."

James 5:14-15 NASB

God demonstrates His concern for our health in many ways. He promises to bless us and answer our prayers. He urges us to seek Him with any needs. And there also are times when He wants to work through other Christians, specifically those called to leadership.

James, a leader in the early church, explained that if anyone was sick, he should *"call for the elders of the church."* These leaders were to gather with the sick, pray for them, and anoint them with oil in the name of the Lord.

This is the *"prayer of faith."* It is the prayer of the Body of Christ standing together on behalf of other Believers. And God promised to act when we obey Him in this way: *"The prayer of faith will save the sick, and the Lord will raise him up."*

We should never place limits on God. He can work in many ways. But we also should remember His concern for the Body of Christ and the power of unity—the power available to us when we pray for each other.

If you have physical needs, obey God's Word and *"call for the elders of the church."* This might be your pastor, elders, church leaders, or others in spiritual authority. Let this kind of prayer build faith, for you and for others who might be sick.

As you or your loved ones face health concerns, continue to pray and believe boldly. Seek God and confess His promises.

Gain from the strength and power that comes as others pray for you. Together, pray the prayer of faith for God's healing power to be released.

PRAYER:
Father, thank You for Your promise to raise the sick through the prayer of faith. Help me to pray for others and to have faith as others pray for me. Thank You. In Jesus' name. Amen.

HEALING KEY:
BELIEVE THAT THE PRAYER OF FAITH WILL RESTORE HEALTH.

DAY 20

Prayer and Confession

"Confess your sins to one another, and pray for one another so that you may be healed. The effective prayer of a righteous man can accomplish much."

James 5:16 NASB

When we are sick or have problems, it's natural to focus on ourselves and our own needs. But James wrote about two keys to healing that may surprise us: (1) confession and (2) praying for others. Both involve the impact other people can have on our lives.

The Bible describes how sin can bind us into harmful lifestyles and habits. Disobeying God can block the flow of His Spirit and keep us from experiencing His presence.

But when we confess our sins, we are freed from the stranglehold of sin. The Bible says there is power when this confession takes place *"to one another."*

Confession changes us in many ways. It helps us be honest with God and gives Him an opportunity to reveal imperfections, weaknesses, and things we may have said or done to displease Him.

Confession also brings us to cleansing, and it leads to changes in our lifestyle. Through cleansing, we are prepared to receive more of God's power, and we're freed from the traps and temptations of the world. Confession can help us stay humble, too.

James also said we should *"pray for one another."* Instead of focusing on ourselves, we are to pray for others! This action helps take our mind off of our own problems, and it helps release God's power in our lives. It helps us think about the Lord and His Kingdom.

Remember these principles if you have health problems. Start by spending time alone with God. Ask Him to search your heart and mind and reveal anything that is displeasing in His sight. Confess your sins, and seek to be clean and pure before Him.

And as you pray, intercede for others who are in need. Cry out to God to heal them or meet their other needs. Then watch to see what the Lord does in your life.

PRAYER:

Father, cleanse me of sin and anything that displeases You. Here are people I know who are in need: _____. Thank You for touching their lives with Your power. In Jesus' name. Amen.

HEALING KEY:

GOD'S POWER IS RELEASED IN OUR LIVES AS WE PRAY FOR OTHERS.

DAY 21

Friends Who Need Healing

"They came, bringing to Him a paralytic, carried by four men. Being unable to get to Him because of the crowd, they removed the roof above Him; and... they let down the pallet on which the paralytic was lying. And Jesus seeing their faith said to the paralytic, 'Son, your sins are forgiven...I say to you, get up, pick up your pallet and go home.'"

Mark 2:3-11 NASB

This is the story of four men who believed that Jesus could heal their paralyzed friend. We don't know if the paralytic believed Jesus could heal him, but his friends did!

They brought him to the home where Jesus was teaching, but it was packed with people and there was no way to enter. Instead of becoming discouraged, these men would not give up. They carried their friend to the roof, dug an opening, and lowered him through that hole.

We can picture Jesus watching as the man was lowered into His presence. Seeing the faith demonstrated by these men, He healed the crippled man and forgave his sins.

All of us know people who have needs. Some are sick. Some have emotional, mental, or financial problems. Some have broken homes and marriages. Some are living in sin. Some simply need salvation.

But regardless of their particular problem, these people need someone to care for them and act with boldness and determination. They need friends with the faith to believe that God can intervene in their circumstances. They need people who believe in miracles, recognizing that nothing is impossible. And they need people who will bring them into the presence of Jesus, determined to get them the help they need.

Today, think about the example of these four men. Who do you know who has serious needs? Who needs a miracle from God? Through compassion and prayer, bring these people to Jesus. Don't give up. If you have faith, you can help change their lives.

PRAYER:

Dear Lord Jesus, here are the names of people who need healing: _____. I believe You for the healing they need. I have faith that You will move in their lives. In Your name. Amen.

HEALING KEY:

MIRACLES HAPPEN TO THOSE WHO DEMONSTRATE FAITH AND PERSISTENCE.

DAY 22

Abiding in Jesus

"Abide in Me, and I in you…he who abides in Me and I in him, he bears much fruit, for apart from Me you can do nothing…If you abide in Me, and My words abide in you, ask whatever you wish, and it will be done for you."

John 15:4-7 NASB

Jesus gave us overwhelming promises, filled with power. One of His most powerful promises was that we can ask whatever we wish, and it will be done for us. Think about this promise: Whatever we wish!

Amazingly, Jesus put no restrictions on what we can ask! Yet we may wonder how many Christians really believe this promise is true. How many have the faith to believe they can ask Him for anything?

But Jesus did provide one condition: This promise only is true for those who *"abide"* in Him. The Greek word here is the key to the passage, occurring 10 times in the span of just seven verses.

This word implies that we must be with Jesus in the same way we "remain" or "continue" in a location. In other words, we must constantly be aware of His presence and conscious that He's with us no matter what we're doing. We need to be so sensitive to Him that we talk with Him and think about Him all the time.

To experience this kind of relationship with Him, our hearts and minds must be filled with His Word. Also, we must allow His Spirit to shape our thoughts and guide our thinking.

Everything changes when we *"abide"* in Him. Dominated by Jesus and His Word, our lives are transformed. Filled with faith, our doubts are banished. We believe His promise that He will grant what we ask.

Today, determine to abide in Jesus as never before. He is with you, right now. Talk with Him. Confess His Word. Be bold in prayer. Dare to *"ask whatever you wish,"* and believe that *"it will be done for you."*

PRAYER:

Dear Lord Jesus, help me to abide in You today. Obeying Your Word, I ask for these things: _____. Thank You that I can ask You for anything. In Your name. Amen.

HEALING KEY:

ABIDE IN JESUS, THEN BOLDLY MAKE YOUR REQUESTS IN PRAYER.

DAY 23

The Fruit of Absolute Trust

"Trust in the LORD with all your heart and do not lean on your own understanding. In all your ways acknowledge Him, and He will make your paths straight. Do not be wise in your own eyes; fear the LORD and turn away from evil. It will be healing to your body and refreshment to your bones."

Proverbs 3:5-8 NASB

Everything changes when we trust in God. This trust leads to a balanced, productive life—a life filled with health and healing.

As we seek God and trust in Him, we develop healthier habits. Our bodies are refreshed, and our minds think more clearly. We have a more intimate relationship with Him, giving us greater boldness in prayer.

Without this trust, our lives can be filled with stress and worry. We can be overcome with doubt and anxiety. We can be uncertain and insecure. Lack of trust in God can lead to negative emotions, such as jealousy and anger. We can become defensive, self-centered, and discouraged.

At the same time, we must avoid trusting in the wrong things or people. We can be deceived into seeking the wrong goals or trapped by Satan's tricks and the empty promises of the world.

Today, think about your life. How much do you trust God? Do you really believe that His Word is true? Trusting in Him means recognizing that He's a lot bigger than any problem or sickness you face. It means believing that He will direct you and meet your needs, just as He promised.

Absolute trust will bring peace to your heart and mind. It will lead to contentment and fulfillment. It will help you be confident and secure in every situation.

Make sure that you put your faith and trust in God. Let Him remove your worries and flood you with peace. Watch as He unleashes His power and brings you new health. Put Him to the test and place your trust in Him… absolutely!

PRAYER:

Father, I commit my life to You. I believe that You want me to prosper and be in health. Thank You for bringing complete health to my body, soul, and spirit. In Jesus' name. Amen.

HEALING KEY:

TRUST IN GOD, AND LET HIM DIRECT YOUR LIFE AND GIVE YOU HEALTH.

DAY 24

God's Promise of Health

"While being reviled, He did not revile in return; while suffering, He uttered no threats, but kept entrusting Himself to Him who judges righteously; and He Himself bore our sins in His body on the cross, so that we might die to sin and live to righteousness; for by His wounds you were healed."

1 Peter 2:23-24 NASB

The Bible is clear: God wants us to be in health and to prosper (3 John 1:2). This isn't an afterthought or something to happen only occasionally. No! This is central to His desire for each of us as His children.

We see this promise in action when the children of Israel were leaving Egypt. God told them, *"I am the LORD who heals you."* He promised to free them from diseases. But this only would happen if they diligently heeded His voice, did *"what is right in His sight,"* listened to His commandments, and kept His statutes (Exodus 15:26). David, too, experienced God's healing power and wrote, He *"heals all your diseases"* (Psalm 103:3).

Throughout His ministry, Jesus consistently demonstrated that God desires His people to be healthy. As He *"went about all the cities and villages,"* He healed *"every sickness and every disease among the people"* (Matthew 9:35). And Peter reminded us of the promise from Isaiah 53 that by His *"stripes you were healed"* (v. 24 NKJV). It's already a fact!

Today, you may have a health issue or some other problem that seems to have no solution. Confess God's promises and declare them to be true in your life. Don't let the devil or the world deprive you of what God has promised. Confess health, and receive His healing.

Call out to Him right now. He is the God who heals all your diseases. Jesus came that you might *"have life"* and *"have it more abundantly"* (John 10:10). Don't let doubt keep you from experiencing the good health God wants you to have. Have faith in Him, and receive His healing touch and abundant life.

PRAYER:
Father, thank You that Jesus died for me. By His stripes I am healed! I believe You for health in my life and the lives of these people I love: _____. Thank You! In Jesus' name. Amen.

HEALING KEY:
JESUS DIED SO YOU COULD BE FORGIVEN AND HEALED.

DAY 25

Exercising God's Authority

"Behold, I give you the authority to trample on serpents and scorpions, and over all the power of the enemy, and nothing shall by any means hurt you."

Luke 10:19 NKJV

The disciples watched as Jesus healed the sick and cast out demons. But one day He said it was time for them to start doing this work. He gave them authority and everything else they needed to carry out this ministry in His name.

Jesus sent out 70 disciples to *"heal the sick"* and proclaim the Kingdom of God. He warned them to expect resistance, but to realize they were going in His name and with His authority: *"He who hears you hears Me, he who rejects you rejects Me, and he who rejects Me rejects Him who sent Me"* (v. 16).

When they returned, they were filled with joy, overwhelmed that *"even the demons are subject to us in Your name"* (v. 17). What Jesus had said was true! He had given them delegated authority—the authority to act in His name—and they had seen His power work through them.

Today, that same power and authority is available to you. Think of all the lives you can touch and impact. You simply need to believe, obey Him, and take action to use the authority you have in His name!

Ask God to give you a fresh revelation of the power and authority He's already given you. Go forward boldly to touch lives and proclaim God's Kingdom. Be spiritually violent and use this authority to shake the world for the Gospel. Instead of being afraid or timid, you can be confident He will bless and protect you. Remember His promise: *"Nothing shall by any means hurt you!"*

Remember that you cannot succeed in your own strength. Simply believe His Word and move forward in faith, ministering in His name. Great rewards await you when you obey. Joy! Fulfillment! Healing! And the satisfaction of seeing lives changed by the power of God.

PRAYER:

Father, thank You for the authority You've given me. I declare Your authority to be true in my life. May Your power flow through me to change this world. In Jesus' name. Amen.

HEALING KEY:

BOLDLY USE THE AUTHORITY GOD HAS GIVEN YOU.

DAY 26

Today's Bible Reading: *Luke 18*
Persistent Prayer

"There was a judge who did not fear God and did not respect man. There was a widow in that city, and she kept coming to him…he said to himself, 'Even though I do not fear God nor respect man, yet because this widow bothers me, I will give her legal protection, otherwise by continually coming she will wear me out.'"

Luke 18:2-5 NASB

This judge was a strong, opinionated man. He wasn't concerned about God or influenced by the opinions of other people. But he faced a challenge from an unlikely source: a seemingly insignificant widow who wanted him to give her *"legal protection."*

The judge had no intention of granting her request, but she would not stop petitioning him. Eventually, she *"wore out"* the judge, who concluded, *"This woman is driving me crazy"* (v. 5 NLT). Because she was persistent, she received the answer she sought.

Jesus told this story to teach the *"need for constant prayer"* and to show us that we *"must never give up"* (v. 1 NKJV). This is how we're to approach God in prayer. Jesus urged us to pray like this widow, persistently pleading with God *"day and night."*

You may be reluctant to show this kind of unrelenting persistence. But this was Jesus' command about prayer! Perhaps there are many reasons you feel like giving up. Your situation may seem hopeless and unchangeable. It may seem that your problems can't be solved.

Yet God wants you to be aggressively persistent. Allow the Holy Spirit to rise within you so you can say, "God, I've had enough. Whatever it takes, I will not be content until this situation is changed. I will pound on the door of Heaven until You answer!"

Don't be afraid to be aggressive. You are obeying Jesus!

You don't have to live in defeat or tolerate sin, poverty, or sickness. Be persistent in your prayers. Never give up until you receive an answer. That is God's command!

PRAYER:
Father, I will not give up, but will seek You until I receive an answer to my situation. Here are my needs: _____. I believe that You will answer my prayers. In Jesus' name. Amen.

HEALING KEY:
PRAY PERSISTENTLY, AND NEVER GIVE UP.

DAY 27

Prepared for Action

"The disciples came to Jesus privately and said, 'Why could we not drive it out?'…'Because of the littleness of your faith; for truly I say to you, if you have faith the size of a mustard seed, you will say to this mountain, "Move from here to there," and it will move; and nothing will be impossible to you. But this kind does not go out except by prayer and fasting.'"

Matthew 17:19-21 NASB

The disciples were puzzled and confused. A man had brought his son to them, but they were unable to cast out the demon that afflicted his life. Why, they wondered, could they not deliver this boy? Jesus told them it was because of their unbelief.

They just needed faith the size of a mustard seed. If they would put their Seed of faith into action, He said, *"Nothing will be impossible for you."*

They failed, but Jesus succeeded. In explaining why, He taught the disciples that *"this kind does not go out except by prayer and fasting."* Clearly, the disciples lacked in this area.

Jesus' life was filled with prayer and fasting. He always was ready for ministry…always filled with power…always ready to battle demons…and always ready to heal the sick.

The Bible defines faith as *"the assurance of things hoped for, the conviction of things not seen"* (Hebrews 11:1). Faith helps us recognize a world that we can only see with spiritual eyes. The Bible tells us that *"faith comes from hearing, and hearing by the word of Christ"* (Romans 10:17). That means our faith is made stronger when we are filled with the Word.

If you want to have power, fill your life with God's Word: Know the Word. Confess the Word. Act on the Word.

Spend time in God's presence. Fast as He leads you. Let Him reveal spiritual truths to you. Let His Spirit empower you for service and give you the faith to release His power!

PRAYER:

Father, help me to see the world through eyes of faith and then put my faith into action. Fill me with Your Spirit. I believe that nothing is impossible with You. In Jesus' name. Amen.

HEALING KEY:

KNOW THE WORD, DEVELOP THE DISCIPLINE OF PRAYER, AND EXERCISE YOUR FAITH.

DAY 28

God Restores Our Health

"I will extol You, O LORD, for You have lifted me up, and have not let my enemies rejoice over me. O LORD my God, I cried to You for help, and You healed me."

Psalm 30:1-2 NASB

The psalmist faced many problems. But looking back, he realized the many ways God had blessed him in the past. He had faced danger, but God rescued him. He had been surrounded by enemies, but God gave him victory. He had faced crises that seemed hopeless, but God brought him *"up from the grave"* (v. 3 NKJV). He had been sick, but when he cried out to God, he was restored to complete health.

Our perspective on the challenges we face can change when we reflect on God's goodness to us, looking back at the problems we've faced and remembering His faithfulness. Without this perspective, we can feel defeated or discouraged. Circumstances in our life can seem hopeless. But confessing God's faithfulness reminds us God's Word is true and He is always with us.

Today, you may be facing many kinds of problems—problems with your health, your finances, your job, or your relationships. You may need direction and face tasks that seem overwhelming. You may be surrounded by enemies who want to harm you.

Today, instead of focusing on your problems, spend a few moments looking back at God's faithfulness in your life. As you think about the problems you've faced in the past, remember what God has done for you, and think about the ways He has met your needs.

God's power is not limited! He still can heal, deliver, save, and provide.

Right now, don't react to your problems with fear, worry, or doubt. Start praising God and committing your problems to Him. He is the God who protects you and provides for you. He is the God who heals you and restores your health. Call on Him. He is waiting to hear from you!

PRAYER:
Father, thank You for all You've done for me. I commit these needs to You: _____. Thank You for restoring my health, rescuing me, and guiding me. In Jesus' name. Amen.

HEALING KEY:
FILL YOUR LIFE WITH PRAISE FOR ALL THAT GOD HAS DONE FOR YOU.

DAY 29

Who Can Pray?

"He gave some as apostles, and some as prophets, and some as evangelists, and some as pastors and teachers, for the equipping of the saints for the work of service, to the building up of the body of Christ."

Ephesians 4:11-12 NASB

Some Christians seem reluctant to pray for healing. They may lack faith or be afraid. They may feel inadequate or lack the confidence that God can use them. Others simply feel that praying for the sick (and performing other aspects of ministry) can only be done by pastors, evangelists, and other full-time Christian workers.

Clearly, each of us has a special calling from God, and some have special ministry gifts. But the Bible declares that ministry is to be done by *"the saints"*—that means every Believer. Each one of us is a minister!

We all can engage in ministry because God empowers us by His Spirit. As Jesus said, His followers *"receive power when the Holy Spirit has come upon you"* (Acts 1:8). On the Day of Pentecost (Acts 2), the Spirit fell on people of all backgrounds, and the early church demonstrated that the Spirit's power enabled them to impact lives. These ordinary, untrained men and women spoke with great boldness, healed the sick, and performed miracles.

Yes, there were clear divisions of responsibility, yet everyone was involved in ministry. We see this truth in the lives of Stephen and Philip, men called to be deacons—to *"serve tables"* and do other practical work (Acts 6:5). Yet both Stephen (Acts 6:8) and Philip (Acts 8:4) were active in ministry. They were willing servants, surrendered to the Spirit, available and ready to be used in the lives of others.

Today, remember that no matter what specific gifts and talents you've been given, God can use YOU to share the Gospel, pray for the sick, and be His minister. Don't be afraid to step out in faith. Surrender to God's Spirit, and let Him use you!

PRAYER:

Father, fill me anew with Your Spirit. Give me boldness and power. I am Your servant. I surrender my life to You. Use me to impact lives with the Gospel. In Jesus' name. Amen.

HEALING KEY:

YOU CAN MINISTER IN THE POWER OF THE HOLY SPIRIT.

DAY 30

Nothing Is Impossible With God

"'You will conceive in your womb and bear a son, and you shall name Him Jesus...The Holy Spirit will come upon you, and the power of the Most High will overshadow you.'...'For nothing will be impossible with God.'"

Luke 1:31-37 NASB

To Mary, the words of the angel Gabriel made no sense. He told her she would give birth to the Son of God. But she didn't understand how this could be possible. How could she, a virgin, have a child? But the angel's message was based on a fundamental truth that would change her life: God could do anything! His power has no limits.

Gabriel defined this power with a double negative. He challenged Mary to name something that was impossible! Clearly, boldly, he stated that *"nothing will be impossible with God."*

Today, God gives you this same challenge. Do you (or someone you know) face a serious health issue? Is there a disease you need to defeat? Do you have a problem that seems impossible to solve? Do you feel overwhelmed or outnumbered? Have you been given a task that seems beyond your capacity? A hurdle that must be overcome?

In each of these situations, think about the words spoken by Gabriel: *"Nothing will be impossible with God."* There is nothing you can name or think of that is impossible for the Lord. All you need is faith, even faith the size of a mustard seed.

Ask God to set you free from limits. Don't be bound by your finite understanding. Instead, realize that He's the Creator. He made the world, and everything is subject to Him. Draw closer to Him, and fill your life with His Word. Confess His promises, and learn to think like He thinks. Then believe Him to release His power in your life—bringing you healing, peace, provision, and restoration.

PRAYER:

Father, I believe that nothing is impossible for You. I commit the following needs to You: _____. Help me exercise faith and remove any limits I've placed on You. In Jesus' name. Amen.

HEALING KEY:

IN EVERY SITUATION, REMEMBER THAT NOTHING IS IMPOSSIBLE WITH GOD!

DAY 31

It Is Finished

"When Jesus had received the sour wine, He said, 'It is finished!'
And bowing His head, He gave up His spirit."

John 19:30 NKJV

In the last words He spoke on the Cross, Jesus declared, *"It is finished."* What exactly was "finished"? Jesus didn't just accomplish a few things—He accomplished everything!

By the Cross, Jesus brought us freedom and forgiveness! Paul wrote that Jesus has made us *"alive together with Him."* Because of His death, all of our sins have been forgiven! Jesus has *"wiped out the handwriting of requirements that was against us...And He has taken it out of the way, having nailed it to the cross."*

Through the Cross, Jesus defeated the forces of Satan and achieved an eternal, spiritual victory over them. As Paul wrote, *"Having disarmed principalities and powers, He made a public spectacle of them, triumphing over them in it"* (Colossians 2:13-15).

On the Cross, He also provided for the healing of our bodies. Isaiah wrote, *"He was wounded for our transgressions, He was bruised for our iniquities; the chastisement for our peace was upon Him, and by His stripes we are healed"* (Isaiah 53:5). Citing Isaiah, Peter went on to say that Jesus *"bore our sins in His body on the cross, so that we might die to sin and live to righteousness"* (1 Peter 2:24).

Even though Jesus said it is *"finished,"* many Christians still have questions and doubts. They're not really sure what they believe. They live as though the battle hasn't yet been won, and they allow their lives to be dominated by defeat, sin, and sickness.

How about you? Are you still living in defeat? Do you still have doubts and worries? Now is the time to turn your life around. Say aloud, *"It is finished!"* Nothing more needs to be done...except you must accept Jesus' finished work.

Today, accept the forgiveness and healing He's already provided for you. You can live in victory!

PRAYER:

Father, thank You for the finished work Jesus did on the Cross for me. I accept Your forgiveness, Your cleansing, and Your healing! I am complete in Jesus. In His name. Amen.

HEALING KEY:

DECLARE "IT IS FINISHED" AND ACCEPT JESUS' WORK ON THE CROSS FOR YOU!

Questions and Answers on Healing

Q: Does God really want to heal you?

A: This important question was asked one day by a leper who approached Jesus for healing:

> Now a leper came to Him, imploring Him, kneeling down to Him and saying to Him, "If You are willing, You can make me clean." Then Jesus, moved with compassion, stretched out His hand and touched him, and said to him, "I AM willing; be cleansed." As soon as He had spoken, immediately the leprosy left him, and he was cleansed (Mark 1:40-42).

Just as Jesus was willing to heal this leper, He is willing to heal YOU!

Many other verses describe Jesus' willingness and ability to heal ALL kinds of diseases and EVERYONE who came to Him:

> Jesus went about all Galilee, teaching in their synagogues, preaching the gospel of the kingdom, and healing all kinds of sickness and all kinds of disease among the people. Then His fame went throughout all Syria; and they brought to Him all sick people who were afflicted with various diseases and torments, and those who were demon-possessed, epileptics, and paralytics; and He healed them (Matthew 4:23-24).

> Great multitudes followed Him, and He healed them all (Matthew 12:15).

> When the sun was setting, all those who had any that were sick with various diseases brought them to Him; and He laid His hands on every one of them and healed them (Luke 4:40).

Jesus' life displayed God's will in action, and His healing power is still available to you today:

> Beloved, I pray that you may prosper in all things and be in health, just as your soul prospers (3 John 1:2).

Q: Where does sickness come from?

A: Disease was not a part of God's original creation, for everything He created was "very good" (Genesis 1:31). There was no sickness on the earth until there was sin on the earth—and this didn't happen until Adam and Eve disobeyed God in Genesis 3. In the beginning, the Garden of Eden had no sin, sickness, or death.

The Bible makes it clear that God doesn't want His people to be sick, but disease is part of the curse of sin and something initiated by the devil:

God anointed Jesus of Nazareth with the Holy Spirit and with power, who went about doing good and healing all who were oppressed by the devil, for God was with Him (Acts 10:38).

While some disease is simply a by-product of living in a fallen world, Jesus at times attributed sickness to a demonic spirit or *"spirit of infirmity"* (Luke 13:10-17). One important aspect of His mission—and the mission of His church—is to destroy the devil's works, and this includes providing people with healing and deliverance:

For this purpose the Son of God was manifested, that He might destroy the works of the devil (1 John 3:8).

As you go, preach, saying, "The kingdom of heaven is at hand." Heal the sick, cleanse the lepers, raise the dead, cast out demons (Matthew 10:7-8).

Q: Is someone's sickness always the result of their personal sin?

A: No. Jesus addressed this issue in John 9:1-7, when He was asked by His disciples why a man was born blind: *"Neither this man nor his parents sinned, but that the works of God should be revealed in him."*

However, it's also true that a person's sin may at times play a role in causing them to be sick:

The prayer of faith will save the sick, and the Lord will raise him up. And IF he has committed sins, he will be forgiven. Confess your trespasses to one another, and pray for one another, that you may be healed (James 5:15-16).

Jesus told the man healed at the Pool of Bethesda, "See, you have been made well. Sin no more, lest a worse thing come upon you" (John 5:14).

Q: Is our physical health related to our spiritual and emotional health?

A: Yes, the Bible describes humankind as having three components—spirit, soul (mind, will, and emotions), and body (1 Thessalonians 5:23-24, Romans 12:1-2, 3 John 1:2, Mark 2:8-12). These are all interrelated, and the Greek word for salvation (sozo) means wholeness and restoration in every part of our being.

Q: Is God's healing power a part of His provision in the atonement?

A: Yes, several verses refer to the connection between Jesus' atonement on the Cross for our sins and His atonement for our sicknesses:

Surely He has borne our griefs
And carried our sorrows;

Yet we esteemed Him stricken,
Smitten by God, and afflicted.
But He was wounded for our transgressions,
He was bruised for our iniquities;
The chastisement for our peace was upon Him,
And by His stripes we are healed (Isaiah 53:4-5).

[Christ] Himself bore our sins in His own body on the tree, that we, having died to sins, might live for righteousness—by whose stripes you were healed (1 Peter 2:24).

Note that receiving a healing touch from God is not a matter of our personal worthiness—if so, none of us would ever be healed. Instead, we come to God for healing (or any other blessing) on the merit of Christ's worthiness and what He did for us on the Cross.

Q: **Can God really heal ALL of our sicknesses?**

A: Some people believe that God only heals some diseases, some of the time—but the Gospels describe Jesus healing everyone who came to Him in faith: *"Great multitudes followed Him, and He healed them all"* (Matthew 12:15).

Even in the Old Testament, David wrote:

Bless the LORD, O my soul,
  And forget not all His benefits:
Who forgives all your iniquities,
  Who heals ALL your diseases,
Who redeems your life from destruction,
  Who crowns you with lovingkindness and tender mercies,
Who satisfies your mouth with good things,
  So that your youth is renewed like the eagle's
(Psalm 103:2-5).

Q: **What methods does God use to bring us healing?**

A: We cannot prescribe how or when the Lord will heal us, but we simply must have our heart open to His promise to make us whole—however and whenever He chooses to do it. People in the Bible were often given specific instructions on what they must do in order to be healed:

- The children of Israel were healed of snake bites by looking at a bronze snake on a pole (Numbers 21:4-9).

- Naaman was healed of leprosy by obeying Elisha's instructions to dip seven times in the Jordan River (2 Kings 5:1-14).

- A blind man was healed when Jesus spit on the dirt, put mud in his eyes, and told him to go and wash in the Pool of Siloam (John 9:1-7).

- The apostles sometimes sent out handkerchiefs or pieces of cloth to those who needed healing (Acts 19:11-12).

- As part of the Great Commission, Jesus said His followers would *"lay hands on the sick, and they will recover"* (Mark 16:15-18).

- God sometimes heals His people as they take Holy Communion (1 Corinthians 11:17-34).

- When we are sick, the Bible instructs us to *"call for the elders of the church,"* to receive prayer and be anointed with oil (James 5:14).

- Luke is described as *"the beloved physician"* (Colossians 4:14), which seems an indication that God often uses doctors and medical science as part of the healing process.

- The Bible gives a number of insights about healthy food and hygiene. For example, it speaks of using *"leaves for medicine"* (Ezekiel 47:12) and having God take away sickness by blessing our bread and our water (Exodus 23:25).

This is only a partial list of all the ways God can work to bring us His healing touch. But the key is to listen for His specific instructions to remedy our situation.

Q: What role does Scripture play in our healing?

A: Standing on God's promises is a key component of receiving His healing power:

He sent His word and healed them, and delivered them from their destructions (Psalm 107:20).

My son, give attention to my words…for they are life to those who find them, and health to all their flesh (Proverbs 4:20-22).

In Exodus 15:26, the Lord promises to be our Healer (literally our Doctor) if we listen to His voice and heed His commands:

If you diligently heed the voice of the LORD your God and do what is right in His sight, give ear to His commandments and keep all His statutes, I will put none of the diseases on you which I have brought on the Egyptians. For I am the LORD who heals you.

In Leviticus 11, 13:1-46, 14:1-32, 16:1-33, God gives instructions for healthy living and the treatment of disease.

Some people erroneously teach that God's power to heal and perform other miracles is no longer available to Believers today. But the Bible says just the opposite, assuring us that all the Lord's promises are still valid for us today: *"All the promises of God in Him are Yes, and in Him Amen, to the glory of God through us"* (2 Corinthians 1:20); *"Jesus Christ is the same yesterday, today, and forever"* (Hebrews 13:8).

Jesus told His disciples: *"Most assuredly, I say to you, he who believes in Me, the works that I do he will do also; and greater works than these he will do, because I go to My Father"* (John 14:12).

Q: What role does spiritual authority have in healing?

A: In the story of Jesus' healing of the centurion's servant (Luke 7:1-10), we see that healing often comes as a direct result of exercising our delegated spiritual authority. Because Jesus was under the authority of the Father, He could just *"say the word"* and heal the centurion's servant—even without being physically present at the servant's side.

In the same way, Jesus delegates HIS authority to US:

As the Father has sent Me, I also send you (John 20:21).

The early church was keenly aware that their power to heal the sick and do other miracles was the direct result of their spiritual authority in Jesus' name. For example, in healing the lame man at the temple gate, Peter said, *"In the NAME of Jesus Christ of Nazareth, rise up and walk"* (Acts 3:6)…*"His name, through faith in His name, has made this man strong, whom you see and know. Yes, the faith which comes through Him has given him this perfect soundness in the presence of you all"* (Acts 3:16). Also see Acts 4:10 and 4:29-31.

Q: What role do Covenant Living and obedience play in our healing?

A: Deuteronomy 28:1-6 and many other passages describe the blessings we can receive as God's people when we listen to His voice and obey Him. However, later in that same chapter, God warns that those who disobey Him will experience sickness, mental illness, fear, confusion, anguish, and restlessness (vs. 15-29, 47-48, 58-67).

Q: How do our attitudes affect our health and healing?

A: There is a direct relationship between our attitudes and our emotional and physical health:

A merry heart does good, like medicine,
But a broken spirit dries the bones (Proverbs 17:22).

A merry heart makes a cheerful countenance,
But by sorrow of the heart the spirit is broken...
He who is of a merry heart has a continual feast (Proverbs 15:13-15).

Q: Is healing always immediate?

A: No, even Jesus once had to touch a blind man twice in order to have his sight totally restored:

He came to Bethsaida; and they brought a blind man to Him, and begged Him to touch him. So He took the blind man by the hand and led him out of the town. And when He had spit on his eyes and put His hands on him, He asked him if he saw anything. And he looked up and said, *"I see men like trees, walking."* Then He put His hands on his eyes again and made him look up. And he was restored and saw everyone clearly (Mark 8:22-25).

Although the Bible tells numerous stories of people who received immediate healings, it also notes that some Believers experienced sickness for a time and had to wait for their healing. For example, Epaphroditus (Philippians 2:25), Timothy (1 Timothy 5:23), Trophimus (2 Timothy 4:20), and Paul (2 Corinthians 12:7-10).

Q: What factors block God's healing power in our lives?

A: The Bible lists a variety of factors that will hinder the release of God's healing power. These include unbelief, unforgiveness, pride, disobedience, poor choices, fear, anxiety, and stress.

Some people, like King Asa, are sick or even die because they fail to seek the Lord for healing: *"Asa became diseased in his feet, and his malady was severe; yet in his disease he did not seek the LORD, but the physicians. So Asa rested with his fathers"* (2 Chronicles 16:12-13).

Q: What role does our desperate determination have in receiving a healing?

A: Many Biblical stories illustrate the importance of perseverance in our prayers for healing (or for any other breakthrough from God):

- Naaman wouldn't have been healed if he had only dipped in the Jordan a few times (2 Kings 5).
- It took diligence for the paralyzed man's friends to dig a hole in the roof and get him to Jesus (Luke 5:17-26).
- The woman with the hemorrhage had to press through the crowd with determination (Mark 5:25-34).
- Bartimaeus faced the anger of the crowd when he cried out for Jesus to heal him, yet he persisted (Mark 10:46-52).

Q: Are you READY to be healed today?

A: Jesus recognized that not everyone is ready to receive their healing. Amid a crowd of sick people waiting at the Pool of Bethesda, He asked a man: *"Do you want to be made well?"* (John 5:6) He's asking YOU the same question today.

The Bible is filled with references to faith being something we must exercise "now" and "today":

NOW faith is the substance of things hoped for, the evidence of things not seen (Hebrews 11:1).

In an acceptable time I have heard you, and in the day of salvation I have helped you. Behold, NOW is the accepted time; behold, NOW is the day of salvation (2 Corinthians 6:2).

One day Jesus went into a synagogue and quoted from Isaiah 61:1-2—saying it was being fulfilled "TODAY." He said the anointing of God's Spirit had come to *"heal the brokenhearted, to proclaim liberty to the captives and recovery of sight to the blind, to set at liberty those who are oppressed"* (Luke 4:16-21).

If you need God's healing touch "Now" and "Today," turn to page 7 for six specific steps you can take to receive your healing!